# REPTILES

## Animal Group Science Book For Kids
## Children's Zoology Books Edition

SPEEDY
PUBLISHING

Reptiles are animals that
are cold-blooded. The
first reptiles are believed
to have evolved around
320 million years ago.

Alligators are closely related to crocodiles. An alligator is distinguished by its wide, rounded snout and black color.

Alligators have been living on Earth for millions of years and are sometimes described as living fossils.

Tortoises are found mainly in Asia and Africa, but also in America. It has a rounder, bumpier, heavier shell than a turtle.

A tortoise's shell is made up of 60 different bones all connected to each other. The top of a tortoise's shell is called a carapace.

Komodo dragons are the largest lizards. They can grop up to 10 feet in length. The Komodo Dragon is covered with a scaly skin.

Komodo dragons are carnivores. They can eat prey that weighs 80% of their own weight.

Chameleon
is a type of
lizard. These
colorful lizards
are known as
one of the few
animals that
can change
skin color.

Chameleons have unique eyes, which can move separately from each other and achieve visual field of 180 degrees.

Gila monster is a venomous lizard. Gila monster has large teeth with grooves. It can inject toxin only by chewing the tissue of the victim.

Gila monsters are dark grey and covered with orange, pink, red or yellow spots. They can live 20 to 30 years.

Skinks are the second largest group of lizards. They can be found in grasslands, forests, mountains, savannas, deserts and urban areas.

Skinks look roughly like true lizards, but most species have no pronounced neck and their legs are relatively small.

Geckos are lizards that live in hot places. They live in rocky deserts and sparse grasslands.

Geckos are nocturnal creatures. Their eyes are adapted to a low level of light. Geckos are usually brightly colored.

There are 12 species of cobras and they all live in Asia, Africa and India. Cobras hunt mostly at night.

Cobras are famous for the threatening hood at their neck. They spread the hood out when they feel threatened or angry.

Anacondas are the largest and heaviest known snakes. Anacondas make their home in the Amazon jungles of South America.

Anacondas are constrictors. They kill their prey by squeezing it to death.

Visit

**BABY PROFESSOR**
EDUCATION KIDS

# www.BabyProfessorBooks.com

to download Free Baby Professor eBooks
and view our catalog of new and exciting
Children's Books